DOGS SET I

GERMAN SHEPHERDS

Heidi Mathea
ABDO Publishing Company

visit us at
www.abdopublishing.com

Published by ABDO Publishing Company, 8000 West 78th Street, Edina, Minnesota 55439. Copyright © 2011 by Abdo Consulting Group, Inc. International copyrights reserved in all countries. No part of this book may be reproduced in any form without written permission from the publisher. The Checkerboard Library™ is a trademark and logo of ABDO Publishing Company.

Printed in the United States of America, North Mankato, Minnesota.
042010
092010

 PRINTED ON RECYCLED PAPER

Cover Photo: Peter Arnold
Interior Photos: Corbis p. 9; Getty Images pp. 4–5, 10–11, 12, 13, 15; iStockphoto pp. 17, 21; Peter Arnold p. 7; Photolibrary pp. 18, 19

Editor: BreAnn Rumsch
Art Direction & Cover Design: Neil Klinepier

Library of Congress Cataloging-in-Publication Data

Mathea, Heidi, 1979-
  German shepherds / Heidi Mathea.
     p. cm. -- (Dogs)
  Includes index.
  ISBN 978-1-61613-406-8
  1. German shepherd dog--Juvenile literature. I. Title.
  SF429.G37M38 2011
  636.737'6--dc22
                                                    2010013414

CONTENTS

THE DOG FAMILY

Dogs are an important part of our history. They are among the first **domesticated** animals. All dogs descend from the gray wolf. Dogs and wolves still share certain instincts. And, they belong to the same family. This is the family **Canidae**.

Humans have developed more than 400 dog **breeds**. These breeds fill many different roles.

Dog lovers everywhere can find the perfect pet for their needs!

Today, the German shepherd is the second most popular dog in the United States. It makes a loving family pet. The German shepherd is also famous for serving as a police dog.

The German shepherd looks different from other dogs. Still, all dogs are related!

GERMAN SHEPHERDS

The German shepherd is a fairly young **breed**. It originated in 1889. A German named Captain Max von Stephanitz worked with others to create the breed.

The German shepherd arrived in the United States in the early 1900s. In 1908, the **American Kennel Club** recognized the breed.

The German shepherd's ancestors are herding and farm dogs. Like its ancestors, the German shepherd still herds sheep. This breed is also good at many other tasks. Today, it is the leading police, guard, and military dog.

German shepherds also make loving, protective pets. And, they are stiff competition in dog shows!

The German shepherd has earned the respect of people worldwide.

What They're Like

German shepherds are strong yet graceful dogs. These beautiful creatures are great to have around! German shepherds are a good choice for many families. They love children and happily guard their homes and humans.

German shepherds are smart and take well to training. Their intelligence makes them useful on police teams. These alert dogs help police officers catch criminals. German shepherds also help on search and rescue missions. These intelligent dogs help find lost or missing persons.

German shepherds have a
keen sense of smell.

German shepherds have a desire to work and
are faithful companions. They make excellent
service animals for blind or disabled people.
German shepherds are loyal, dependable dogs.

COAT AND COLOR

The German shepherd is a hardworking dog. Its thick double coat keeps it warm and protects it from the sun's rays. This beautiful dog has straight, medium-length hair. Shorter hair covers its head, legs, and paws. Longer, thicker hair grows on the dog's neck.

German shepherds come in various colors. The most common coat colors are black and tan or black and red. These dogs display a black saddle marking on their backs. Their feet and legs are tan or red.

German shepherds can also be sable, solid black, or bicolor. Bicolor German shepherds appear mostly black. They may have small tan patches on their eyebrows. The legs, bellies, and areas under their tails may also have small amounts of tan.

These natural beauties attract many admirers.

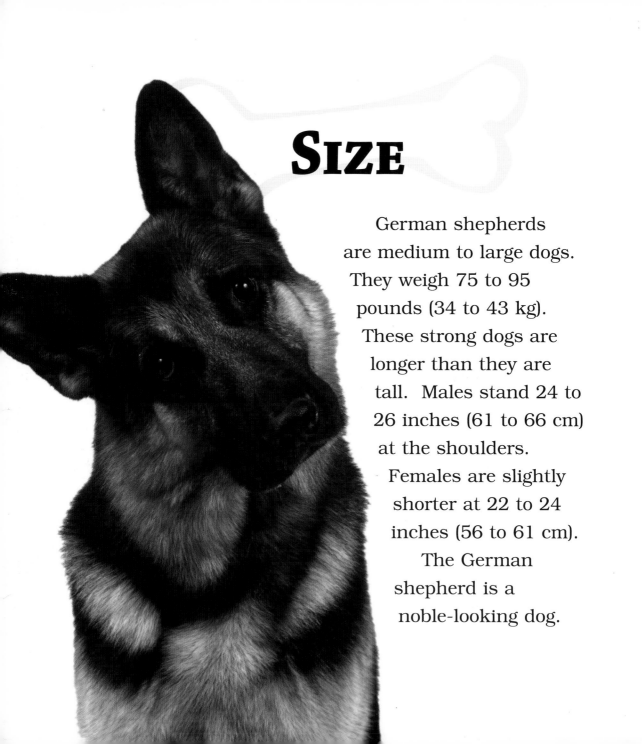

SIZE

German shepherds are medium to large dogs. They weigh 75 to 95 pounds (34 to 43 kg). These strong dogs are longer than they are tall. Males stand 24 to 26 inches (61 to 66 cm) at the shoulders. Females are slightly shorter at 22 to 24 inches (56 to 61 cm). The German shepherd is a noble-looking dog.

Straight, powerful legs support its well-muscled body and deep chest. This dog carries its bushy tail low.

The German shepherd's **muzzle** is shaped like a long wedge. Its ears are large, erect, and turned forward. Its almond-shaped eyes are alert and dark. All of these features give the German shepherd a keen, intelligent look.

These muscular animals move with grace and power.

CARE

German shepherds are amazing dogs, but they are not for everybody. These dogs need to be busy constantly. Daily exercise can help keep them out of mischief.

Regular grooming is important for German shepherds. Their thick double coats **shed** a lot! Daily brushing removes dead hair and keeps their beautiful coats from becoming **matted**. German shepherds need their nails clipped regularly, too.

Like all dogs, German shepherds need veterinary care to stay healthy. A veterinarian can provide **vaccines**. He or she can also **spay** or **neuter** puppies.

An occasional bath will keep your German shepherd clean and sweet smelling.

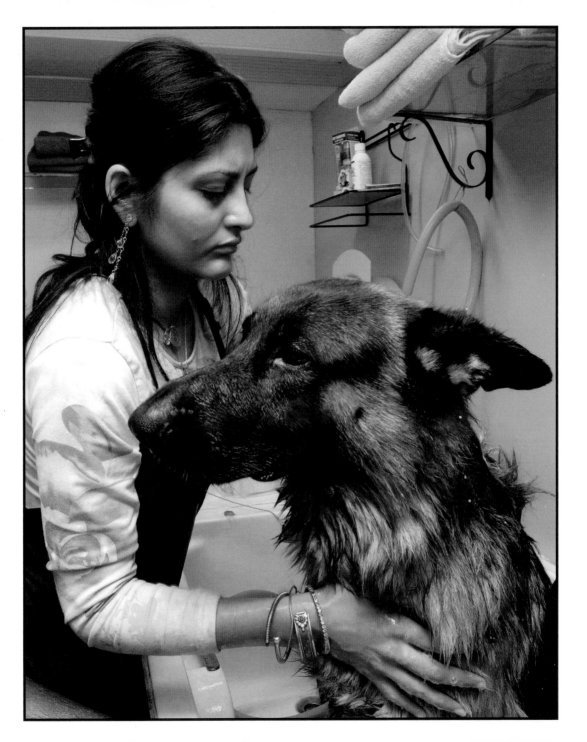

FEEDING

The German shepherd is an active dog and needs a well-balanced diet. A high-quality commercial dog food will provide the proper **nutrients**.

When you buy a puppy, continue with the same food it was eating at the **breeder**'s. A small puppy needs about three meals a day. It will need only two meals by the time it is six months old.

Don't let your pet go thirsty! A constant supply of fresh water is especially important for this energetic breed. Keep water and food next to each other in stainless steel bowls.

German shepherds must be exercised every day so they do not gain weight. Many owners enjoy walking or bicycling with their dogs beside them.

Dogs like schedules, so feed them at the same time every day.

THINGS THEY NEED

German shepherds love to run! A large, fenced yard will keep them safe while playing. But don't leave these active animals alone in the backyard. They want to be with their families. They will react poorly to being separated for extended periods.

After a busy day, a German shepherd needs a quiet place to sleep indoors. A crate or a soft blanket is perfect for a sleepy German shepherd.

German shepherds are high-energy dogs.

German shepherd owners need to buy a few other items for their dogs. These include a leash, a collar, an identification tag, and toys. An identification tag will help someone contact you if your dog becomes lost. Toys keep your active dog from growing bored and chewing your furniture!

Toys will keep your puppy busy and happy!

PUPPIES

Like all dogs, German shepherd mothers are **pregnant** for about nine weeks. At birth, puppies are tiny and completely dependent on their mothers. They begin to see and hear about 10 to 14 days after birth.

Can you offer a German shepherd a good home? If so, look for a reliable **breeder** or a rescue organization.

German shepherds can be hard to handle if they are not properly trained. Training must start the very day you bring your new pet home. This will help the dog grow into a well-adjusted companion.

Over time, introduce your puppy to new people and surroundings. Allowing the dog to make friends will make it a happier pet. German shepherds make loyal family members for 12 to 15 years.

German shepherd puppies are born with their ears lying flat. The ears will begin to come up between two and four months of age. The ears are usually erect by the time the puppies have permanent teeth.

GLOSSARY

American Kennel Club - an organization that studies and promotes interest in purebred dogs.

breed - a group of animals sharing the same ancestors and appearance. A breeder is a person who raises animals. Raising animals is often called breeding them.

Canidae (KAN-uh-dee) - the scientific Latin name for the dog family. Members of this family are called canids. They include domestic dogs, wolves, jackals, foxes, and coyotes.

domesticated - adapted to life with humans.

matted - formed into thick, tangled masses of hair.

muzzle - an animal's nose and jaws.

neuter (NOO-tuhr) - to remove a male animal's reproductive organs.

nutrient - a substance found in food and used in the body. It promotes growth, maintenance, and repair.

pregnant - having one or more babies growing within the body.

shed - to cast off hair, feathers, skin, or other coverings or parts by a natural process.

spay - to remove a female animal's reproductive organs.

vaccine (vak-SEEN) - a shot given to prevent illness or disease.

WEB SITES

To learn more about German shepherds, visit ABDO Publishing Company on the World Wide Web at **www.abdopublishing.com**. Web sites about German shepherds are featured on our Book Links page. These links are routinely monitored and updated to provide the most current information available.

INDEX

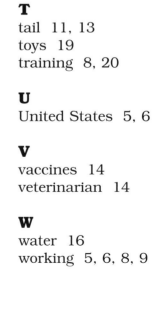

WITHDRAWN

 Indianapolis
Marion County
Public Library

Renew by Phone
269-5222

Renew on the Web
www.imcpl.org

For General Library Information
please call 269-1700